76 Graded Studies for Flute

selected and edited by Paul Harris and Sally Adams

Book One (1-54)

CONTENTS

FABER *ff* MUSIC

INTRODUCTION

In the two books comprising this collection, we have assembled a broad repertoire of study material that covers a wide spectrum of basic technique and provides a firm foundation for progress. The studies have been arranged in order of increasing difficulty, according to a carefully planned technical progression. Book One begins at elementary level, while Book Two takes the students from intermediate to advanced level.

In the main, we have drawn on established study collections by distinguished performers of the 18th and 19th centuries, all of whom made an approach to the diverse problems encountered in the development of technical facility and control. We have also included a number of new, specially composed studies that introduce aspects of 20th-century style and thus extend the scope of the selection.

It is important to identify - perhaps with the assistance of your teacher - the specific purpose of each study and the particular facets of technique it sets out to develop. The following suggestions will be useful.

Breath control Most aspects of tonal control depend on a sustained and concentrated column of air. This is the basis of all *legato* and *staccato* playing, and a means of controlling intonation.

Tone quality It is important to maintain quality and consistency of tone when playing studies, scales and technical exercises.

Dynamics While the actual volume of sound implied by particular dynamic markings may vary from work to work, dynamic relationships within a single study should be constant. *Crescendo* and *diminuendo* should always be carefully graded, increasing or decreasing at a constant rate.

Intonation When practising studies, it is important to test intervals by reference to a tuning fork, piano or electronic tuning device.

Articulation The chosen length and quality of notes should be matched throughout and related to the character of the particular study. An understanding of the various symbol used is necessary.

Finger technique The development of a controlled and coordinated finger movement is the main purpose of the technical study. You should always identify the particular difficulties and seek to acquire the necessary control.

Rhythm These studies should often be practised with a metronome. Where there are rhythmic difficulties, sub-divide the basic pulse. You should always count, but it is important that undue emphasis is not placed on beats, except for a slight feeling for the natural bar accents. These primary and secondary accents should be felt but not over-emphasised.

Character The character and mood of a study should be considered, as these will determine note duration, accentuation, tone-colour and so on.

Metronome markings In most cases we have indicated the *maximum* tempo for each study. You should use your discretion regarding suggested metronome markings.

Breathing indications These are suggestions and need not be strictly observed.

PAUL HARRIS
SALLY ADAMS

© 1994 by Faber Music Ltd
First published in 1994 by Faber Music Ltd
3 Queen Square London WC1N 3AU
Music drawn by Wessex Music Services
Cover design by Shireen Nathoo Design
Printed in England by Caligraving Ltd
All rights reserved

ISBN 0-571-51430-8

To buy Faber Music publications or to find out about the full range of titles available please contact your local music retailer or Faber Music sales enquiries:

Faber Music Limited, Burnt Mill, Elizabeth Way, Harlow, CM20 2HX England
Tel: +44 (0)1279 82 89 82   Fax: +44 (0)1279 82 89 83
sales@fabermusic.com   fabermusic.com

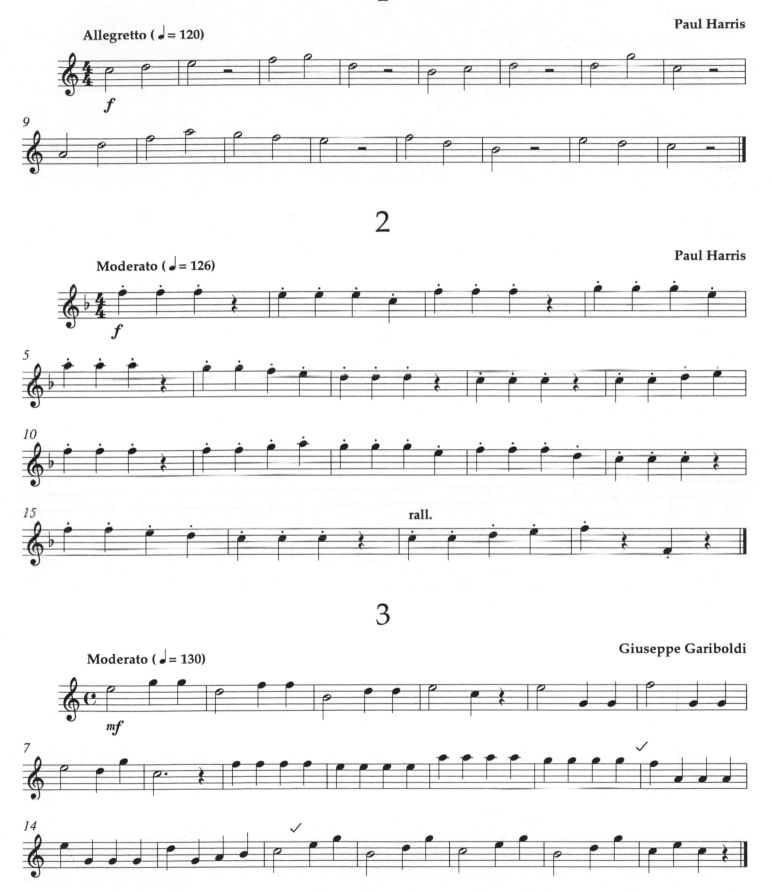

4

Andante (♩ = 92)

Paul Harris

5

Andante con moto (♩ = 108)

Paul Harris

6

Allegretto (♩ = 126)

François Garnier

7

Paul Harris

8

Sally Adams

9

Ernesto Köhler

4

13

Ernesto Köhler

14

Carl Baermann

17

4'Nov

Ernesto Köhler

18

Paul Harris

8

4 Feb.

19
Hessian Dance

Anon.

20
The Sun from the East

Anon.

21

Jeremiah Clarke

22

Giuseppe Gariboldi

23

Andante con moto (♩. = 44)

Marin Marais

24

Gustav Hincke

Tempo giusto (♩ = 120)

25
Two Tunes for the Parrot

Anon.
(pub. 1717)

26

Georg Philipp Telemann

29

Jean-Louis Toulou

14

30

Allegro moderato (♩ = 80)

Giuseppe Gariboldi

31

Lamentarola (♩ = 60)

Anon.

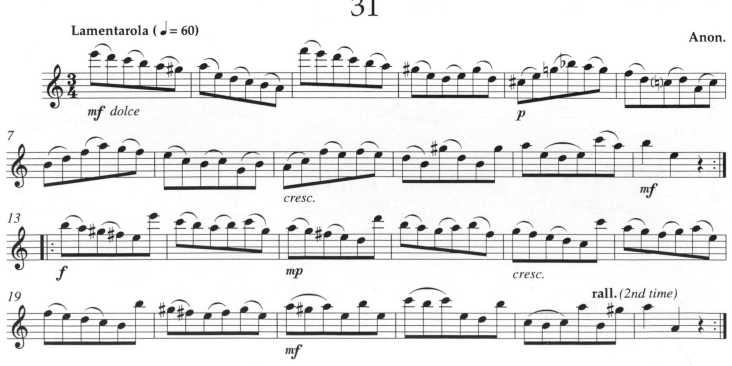

32

Animato (♩ = 144)

Paul Harris

33

Allegro (♩. = 84)

Georg Philipp Telemann

34

Wilhelm Popp

35

Wilhelm Popp

36

Johann Joachim Quantz

37

Giuseppe Gariboldi

26 Nov

38

Paul Harris

39

Anton Bernhard Fürstenau

42

Johann Joachim Quantz

43

Giuseppe Gariboldi

Paul Harris

45

Giuseppe Gariboldi

46

Louis Drouet

47

Wilhelm Popp

70d 14° Oct

48

Largo (♩ = 60)

Anon.

49

Allegro (♩ = 120)

Georg Philipp Telemann

26

50

Maestoso (♩ = 80)

C. Ferling

51

Largo (♪ = 69)

Georg Philipp Telemann

53

Louis Drouet

54

Ernesto Köhler

LIST OF SOURCES

The studies in this book are drawn from the following sources:

Carl Baermann (1811-85)
Vollständige Clarinett-Schule (André, 1864-75)
(14)

Louis Drouet (1792-1873)
Méthode pour la Flûte (Paris, 1837)
(46, 53)

C. Ferling
48 Studies (Breitkopf & Härtel)
(50)

Anton Bernhard Fürstenau (1792-1852)
Flötenschule, Op.42 (Breitkopf & Härtel, 1825)
(39)

Giuseppe Gariboldi (1833-1905)
Methode for Flute (Paris, ?)
(3, 10, 11, 15, 16, 22, 27, 30, 37, 43, 45)

François Garnier (1759-1825)
Studienwerk (Johann André, 1800)
(6, 52)

Gustav Hincke
Praktische Elementarschule (Leipzig, 1888)
(24)

Ernesto Köhler (1849-1907)
Schule für Flöte (Leipzig, 1887)
(9, 13, 17, 54)

Marin Marais (1656-1728)
Les Folies d'Espagne (Paris, 1701)
(12, 23)

Charles Nicholson (1795-1837)
Nicholson's School for the Flute (London, 1836)
(41)

Wilhelm Popp (1828-1903)
Erster Flötenunterricht Op.387 (Leipzig)
(34, 35, 40, 47)

Johann Joachim Quantz (1697-1773)
Solfeggi
(36, 42)

Heinrich Soussmann (1796-1848)
Grosse Praktische Flötenschule Op.53 (Schuberth, 1839)
(28)

Georg Philipp Telemann (1681-1767)
Zwölf Fantasien für Querflöte
(26, 33, 49, 51)

Jean Louis Toulou (1786-1865)
Méthode de Flûte Op.100 (Paris, 1835)
(29)

GLOSSARY OF TERMS

Adagio	Slow	*Lamentoso*	Mournfully
Allegretto	A little slower than *Allegro*	*Largo*	Slowly
Allegro	Lively	*Leggiero*	Lightly
Allegro moderato	Moderately lively	*Maestoso*	Majestically
Andante	At a walking pace	*Martellato*	Hammered
Animato	Animated	*Moderato*	Moderately
A tempo	Resume the original speed	*Molto*	Much, very
Cantabile	In a singing style	*Mosso*	Movement
Con moto	With movement	*Poco*	Little
Crescendo (cresc.)	Becoming louder	*Poco a poco*	Little by little
D.C. al Fine	Return to the start and play as far as *Fine*	*Presto*	Fast
		Quasi	Like
Delicato	Delicately	*Rallentando (rall.)*	Becoming gradually slower
Diminuendo	Becoming softer	*Risoluto*	Resolutely
Double	Variation	*Ritenuto (rit.)*	Held back
Dolce	Sweetly	*Scherzando*	Playfully
Energico	Energetically	*Simile (sim.)*	Similarly
Fine	End	*Spiritoso*	Spirited
Giusto	Appropriately	*Tempo di gavotte*	The speed of a gavotte
Grazioso	Gracefully	*Vigoroso*	Vigorously
Lamentarola	Like a lament	*Vivace*	Fast and lively